GRANADA CATHEDRAL

Aldeasa

THE FOUNDING OF THE CATHEDRAL

In accordance with the Peace Agreement signed by the Catholic Kings and the Moorish King Boabdil, Granada, which became part of the Kingdom of Castile on 2 January 1492, continued to be a Muslim city. However, Christianity, the religion of the victorious side, made its presence felt from the start. As well as consecrating various mosques, a papal bull enabled Cardinal Pedro González de Mendoza, Archbishop of Toledo, to found the church of Santa María de la Encarnación in Granada in 1492 (also founding the cathedrals of Guadix and Almería that same day).

A PERIPATETIC CATHEDRAL

While a permanent building was under construction, the cathedral had three temporary locations. It was first set up in the Royal Mosque of the Alhambra. This building was 60 feet long by 50 feet wide with three aisles. Work was carried out to make it more suitable for its new Christian function. Just a few years later, in 1495, the cathedral moved to a new building in the Jewish quarter. This was a church in the Gothic style with a nave and six chapels on either side. The Archbishop and Chapter moved into living quarters next door.

In 1499 the first rebellion of the Moorish inhabitants of Granada took place. As a punishment they were forced to leave their lands and houses or to convert to Christianity. Almost all chose the second option, and Granada therefore evolved from a Muslim city to a Hispano-moresque one. As a consequence, most of the now redundant mosques were consecrated and converted into churches. It was also decided to move the cathedral to the city's main mosque. Pope Alexander VI, in a document dated 8 October 1502, authorised the move. In addition, out of respect for the Archbishop Hernando de Talavera, who was particularly desirous not to offend the recently converted Muslims, the move was not made until various months after his death on 14 May 1507. The cathedral remained within this mosque-church for more than fifty years until 17 August 1561, when the Chapter moved into the current building, even though it was still under construction.

THE CATHEDRAL

Granada Cathedral was conceived as an expression of the victory of Christianity over Islam. After almost eight centuries of Muslim domination (711-1492), it was seen as just that Christianity should again take hold in this region where it had once been so firmly rooted. For this reason, a cartouche with a Latin inscription was added to one of the Cathedral's doors (the so-called Pardon Door), held up by two figures representing *Faith and Justice*, and reading: "After seven hundred years of Muslim rule, both people acknowledged the Catholic Kings; we buried their bodies in this church and raised their souls to the sky, because they acted with justice and faith. The first priest was Fernando, a model of wisdom, custom and virtuous life".

In addition, the cathedral also had a second, "political" significance: it expressed the Imperial image of Charles V (in a way similar to Charles's palace in the Alhambra),

The Main Chapel. Fernando el Católico in Prayer.

and was also intended as the mausoleum of the Habsburg rulers.

The Construction of the Building

Granada had to have a cathedral "fitting to such an important city". Queen Isabel insisted to the Chapter on its completion, but in her will she only stressed the founding and completion of the funerary chapel. On the death of the Queen, Fernando commissioned the plans for the future cathedral and shortly afterwards Enrique Egas was placed in charge of the project. Work began with the funerary chapel, whose structure was completed in 1517. At the same time, and not without difficulty, adjacent houses were acquired which would be demolished in order to achieve the necessary large plot for the new building. The first stone was laid on 25 March 1523, the festival of the Incarnation. For some years the building followed a plan inspired by Toledo Cathedral. When work stopped in 1528 and Enrique Egas was dismissed, the entire exterior wall had reached ground level and the foundations of the Main Chapel were also laid.

Dissatisfaction with the Gothic design, the intention of building a mausoleum which responded to the imperial grandeur of Charles V (who had expressed the desire to be buried in the cathedral and not in the Royal Chapel, which he described as "more like a merchant's chapel than a king's due to its narrowness and lack of light"), and above all the decision taken by Archbishop Pedro Ramiro de Alba, meant that Diego de Siloé was named chief architect and commissioned to produce a new design.

Siloé respected the dimensions already set out by Egas (115 metres long by 65 metres wide) and proposed an original design with the church divided into two separate areas, the sanctuary and the main body, joined and articulated by a transept which would also function as a separate access route to the Royal Chapel from the outside via the Pardon Door. The circular sanctuary, conceived like a huge shrine, would be both the main chapel and the imperial mausoleum. The body of the cathedral was to be of square form, with a Greek cross in the middle of its five naves, formed from the crossing with the two central naves which were higher than the others, and with a domed ceiling at the intersection (This concept of two different but joined architectural elements can still be seen in the layout of the roofs, but is difficult to appreciate inside the building due to later alterations).

With this design, Siloé abandoned the Gothic plan of five naves (a basilical groundplan with a small presbytery and two ambulatories) and instead juxtaposed two centralised spaces, corresponding to the two forms of the early church – the circular and the Greek cross – which were revived and deployed during the Renaissance (the Counter-reformation saw a return to the basilical plan).

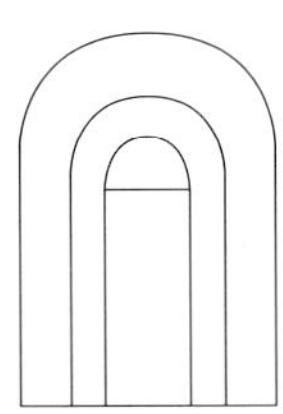

Gothic plan

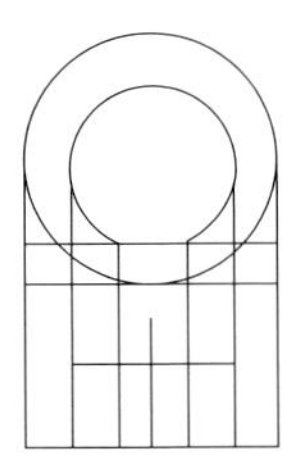

Siloé's plan

The Central Nave seen from the Main Chapel.

On discovering that the new design for the cathedral was "Roman" in style, Charles V expressed concern that it contrasted with the Royal Chapel which was already built in the Gothic style. Siloé himself was sent by the Chapter to Court to defend "his work and ideas". The architect began to set his ideas in motion in 1529 (he had previously made a model to demonstrate that the building could be realised in the new style but still using the structures already built by Egas). During the first ten years he built the sanctuary and the chapels behind it (retaining the Gothic-style ribbed ceilings) and in the following years he constructed the main chapel, which was completed in 1558. Siloé himself directed the design and manufacture of the stained glass windows, drawing a large number of the original designs (again retaining the medieval idea that the filtered light of the coloured glass was intended to created a symbolic darkness, imbued with spirituality). The glass was made by Juan del Campo and Teodoro de Holanda.

When the sanctuary was completed, a wall was built to separate it from the rest of the building and it could then be used to celebrate mass (from 1561), while work on the naves continued. In 1563 Siloé died, having built the sanctuary, built all the walls to ground level and set up the columns of the main body of the building. He was succeeded by his chosen pupil, Juan de Maeda. During Maeda's term of office (1564-76) work proceeded much more slowly, and only the first section of the tower was built. Following numerous failures, disputes with the master of works and court cases, Ambrosio Vico, who had been foreman of work since 1575, took over the project. Vico's role was an important one as he broke away from and changed the course of work which had until then been relatively coherent and in line with Siloé's plans. Vico completed the second section of the tower, built the third, and started the fourth, octagonal element; however, this had to be dismantled shortly afterwards as it threatened to destroy the whole structure. It was reinforced and left incomplete (as it is now). Vico then built the naves of the crossing and the choir and started on the ceilings which were of Gothic type for reasons of safety, rather than Siloé's "Roman" ones. Finally, he continued work on the façade of the Pardon Door, whose lower part had been designed and executed by Siloé. After Vico (who had been acting head from 1582 to 1588 and titular head from 1588 to 1623) the following men held the post: Ginés Martínez (who died shortly after being appointed), Juan de Aranda (who was busy with Jaén cathedral and made no contribution to Granada), Miguel Guerrero (who complete the vaults of the crossing, built the nave immediately parallel and completed the roofs of the chapels on the left), Alonso Cano (who was named head of work for his design for the main façade which departed from Siloé's design, but died the year of his appointment), José Granados de la Barrera (who built the main façade following Alonso Cano's design, and the chapels on the right, leaving half completed the cupola of the crossing of the central nave), Teodoro Ardemans, Melchor de Aguirre, Zurita, Francisco del Castillo (who executed the cupola started by Granados, but so badly that it had to be demolished),

Above, the rose window of the main façade.
Below, the Upper Row of Stained Glass Windows in the Cupola.

Francisco Otero and Francisco Rodríguez (who replaced the cupola with a vault). With the termination of the last vaults in 1704 the cathedral was completed, 181 years after the first stone was laid. Later additions would be decorative ones only.

The Results and their Evaluation

Like so many other important buildings, Granada Cathedral as we see it today is not a single unity created at one time, but the result of a long process of construction: it was started as a late Gothic design, subsequently becoming a Renaissance once (or "in the roman style" to use the contemporary phrase), and then once again acquiring Gothic features in the completion of the vaults, while the main façade is Baroque and the interior decoration followed the tastes of succeeding and prevailing artistic currents. The building also reflects political events, changes of style, institutional problems, religious requirements, and functional changes (the most important of these being the canons' choir which has been sited in four different locations, and the main altar).

Some critics have interpreted the cathedral as a Gothic church in Renaissance guise; others have seen it as an example of the transitional style between Gothic and Renaissance. In fact, it is a Renaissance church, designed by Siloé on a pre-existing Gothic groundplan and later modified in its structure and decoration to make it as much as possible like a medieval church.

The building has aroused contradictory opinions, ranging from its description as a masterpiece, to that of a pile of stone devoid of either taste or proportion.

A GUIDED TOUR AROUND THE BUILDING

The Interior

On entering the Cathedral, the visitor is surprised by the height, the amount of light and the pale tones of the walls.

The height is not normal for a Renaissance building. Siloé achieved it in the main chapel by building two stories plus a raised cupola, and in the naves by setting the whole structure, walls and supports, on a high base and podium and then adding to the tall and finely proportioned first level a second entablature of carved pilasters from which spring the arches of the vault.

The pillars have attached half-columns, which in the case of the free-standing ones where they appear on all four sides, give the appearance of a single column. The lighting of the sanctuary and the main body of the church are different. The sanctuary is rather dim due to the thickness of its walls, and the light which enters is filtered by the colours of the stained glass and the gilding on the walls. In contrast, the lighting of the main body is bright and natural. Was this Siloé's idea or was it achieved by his successors? Given that the latter changed the style of the vaults, returning to the cross-vault type, it may also be that they discarded the idea of stained glass when they developed a different concept of the interior. At that time, natural lighting was favoured for churches and the old idea of the symbolic value of the "non-natural" light created by stained glass no longer existed (in addition, the craft of stained glass making was no longer an integral part of architecture and

The Roofs of the Vaults.

was by this time in decline). In fact, of the 98 windows arranged around the upper walls of the cathedral, 62 are blind and only 36 remain in use and have plain glass. The interior is nonetheless extremely light: natural light fills the naves in contrast to the warm and dimmer lighting of the sanctuary.

The whitewashing of the walls (a layer of dissolved gesso paste which creates the greyish tones) has been explained in various ways: some believe that it was intended as the undercoat for gilding similar to the sanctuary; other state that it is to be found in other buildings of the period and was intended by Diego de Siloé. According to the second opinion, for Renaissance architects whitewashed interiors firstly had a practical value (in this case giving a uniform colour to the various different materials, stone, mortar and brick, as well as giving consistency to the appearance of the stone); secondly, they had an aesthetic value (giving the effect of the grandeur of white marble, as well increasing the sense of luminosity); and thirdly, they had a symbolic and spiritual value (in that the building was designed not to emphasise mystery and spiritual seclusion, as in medieval cathedrals, but to reveal the glory of God and the joy of salvation, expressed in the luminosity of white and gold).

A. *The Sanctuary*

This is the most important area within the whole building. "One of the most remarkable Renaissance sanctuaries in Europe and spatially one of the most important constructions of the period", according to Rosenthal.

Of circular form, it has three concentric areas of different heights: the rotunda, the ambulatory and the radial chapels.

The rotunda, which serves as the Main Chapel of the cathedral, is an impressive cylindrical structure measuring 22 metres diameter by 45 metres high, arranged in two sections with the addition of the semi-circular dome, separated by entablatures with reliefs. The pillars have attached half columns that continue into the ribs of the vault.

Between the columns at the ground floor level are openings leading to the ambulatory. Above their arched tops are rectangular openings that seem to have been intended to house the funerary urns of the monarchs (these openings are currently sealed up and have paintings over them representing *the theological saints* by Atanasio Bocanegra and Juan de Sevilla). In 1612 Baroque consoles were attached to the shafts of the twelve columns to support a series of paintings of *The Apostles*, probably by Martín de Aranda or Bernabé de Gaviria (the *Saint Paul* is by Alonso de Mena).

The second level is also divided into two sections. In the lower part are seven stone altarpieces for which Alonso Cano executed a series of paintings on Marian themes (*the Immaculate Conception, the Nativity, the Presentation, the Incarnation, the Visitation, the Purification,* and *the Assumption*). In the lower part are double windows with fourteen stained glass windows by Teodoro de Holanda which were brought from Antwerp.

At the base of the cupola are ten windows that also have stained glass made in Spain by Juan del Campo (with the exception of the one of *Saint John the Baptist*, which is modern). In 1702 Luca

The Main Chapel.

Giordano and Antonio Palomino were contracted to paint the cupola with a "Glory", but this project was never realised.

The Marian series by Cano is, in the opinion of the art historian Wethey, "unique in the history of Spanish painting. No other group of canvases of this date is so coherent, even though they were painted over a period of ten years." Cano's paintings match the double row of stained glass windows in their sense of volume, luminosity and colour.

Since 1929 the centre of the Main Chapel has housed a *tabernacle* of repoussé silver which stands on a base of serpentine marble with silver reliefs. It was made by Navas Parejo and was donated by the Duke of San Pedro de Galatino. (Diego de Siloé originally placed an altar here covered by a large and delicate canopy which he himself carved and gilded. This would have created the effect of more light in the chapel).

Although a self-contained space, the Main Chapel is also open to the rest of the building. More than half of its overall ground plan is occupied by the area behind where it is connected to the ambulatory by seven large splayed arches; opposite each one of these are the main chapels of the sanctuary, while the smaller ones are aligned opposite the pillars and buttresses, which are themselves arranged to create an intermediary passageway. The other half of the circle opens out onto the main body of the lower church: two columns on either side are joined so that the arch disappears and the two subsequent ones open like door jambs to create a large opening corresponding with the central nave.

In the areas formed by the joined arches are vertical niches with images of *Saint Francis of Assisi*, *Saint Francis Xavier*, *Saint Pedro de Alcántara*, *Saint Domingo de Guzmán*, *Saint Ignatius Loyola*, and *Saint John of God*, each donated to the cathedral by their respective Order.

The ambulatory, or area around the rotunda, has Renaissance style-vaults, which contrast with the cross-vaults in the larger and smaller chapels. In the wall above the chapel arches are 22 stained glass windows also by Teodoro de Holanda and Juan del Campo. In the niches of the ambulatory are paintings which originally came from a single altarpiece, now dismantled, while on the columns is a modern *Calvary series* made up of large Greek crosses by Navas Parejo.

B. *The Main Arch and the Transept*

The unusual repeated tri-partite arrangement of the columns of the rotunda creates the two massive supports for the arch which connects the Main Chapel and the rest of the church. This impressive arch, 32 metres high and 12 metres wide, is unusual in that the soffits are notably narrow in order to maintain the semi-circular form of the cupola.

In these soffits and above the small balconies are sculpted *Figures in prayer* (appropriate to funerary chapels) representing the monarchs *Isabel and Fernando* by Pedro de Mena, dating from the late seventeenth century, replacing those of Charles V and his wife who were going to be buried here. Higher up are tondos with busts of *Adam and Eve* by Alonso Cano. Finally, in the attic level at the top of the arch are two canvases representing *Saint Cecilius* and *Saint James of Compostela* by

The Tabernacle of the Main Altar and Cupola.

Cuadros
Mora
Molduras

AVEMARIA

José Risueño. The two silver ceiling lamps were designed by Alonso Cano and made by the silversmith Diego Cervantes in 1563-64. In the corners of the arch are two marble *pulpits* by Francisco Hurtado Izquierdo made between 1713 and 1717 (the sculptures on them are by Duque Cornejo).

On both sides of the main arch at the termination of the lateral aisles are two altars where the arches function as frames for the altarpieces and are gilded in a way similar to the interior of the Main Chapel. Inset into the altar on the right is a large canvas representing the *Apparition of the Virgin to Saint Bernard* by Atanasio Bocanegra, and above it one of the miracles of Saint Benito by Juan de Sevilla; on the left altar is a canvas depicting the *Flagellation*, also by Sevilla, and above it a *Saint Cecilius* by Bocanegra.

C. *The Main Church*

This has five aisles plus two rows of lateral chapels that connect with the chapels in the sanctuary.

This part of the church, built after Siloé's death, departs from his designs. The ceilings are of cross-vault type, in contrast to the ambulatory ceilings, and the planned cupola was not constructed. In 1620 the Canons' choir was installed in the central, widest nave, and on either side of this, between two columns, the organs made by Francisco Llops. These were replaced in 1749 by the present ones made by Leonardo Dávila. In the mid-seventeenth century a crypt was opened up beneath the choir, to function as a cemetery (the burial place of bishops and canons, and also of María Pineda). Between 1734 and 1741 José de Bada executed and installed a fine red marble altar in the retrochoir. The choir, which acts as a private church for the canons situated in the middle of the aisles, prevented light from entering this area. For this reason, and given that the choirstalls were not of particular artistic merit, it was moved to the Main Chapel in 1929, leaving the central aisle uncluttered. The cathedral thus acquired more space and became more serviceable from a liturgical viewpoint.

D. *The Doorways and Side Chapels*

1. The Doorway and Lower Level of the Tower (the Museum). This door was built by Juan de Maeda in 1665. Above the arch are reliefs of *Justice and Prudence accompanied by two children holding up cartouches.* In the centre of the second level is a high relief of *Charity* by Diego Pesquera dating from 1565. This door gives access to the ground floor of the tower. It was used as the Chapter House between 1713 and 1928. Here the Cathedral Museum is provisionally installed, comprising a display of numerous pieces of goldsmith's work, sculptures, paintings and liturgical ornaments (some pieces of great value).

2. The Chapel of the Virgin Pilar. This was decorated by Francisco Aguado between 1782 and 1785 for the burial of Archbishop Antonio Jorge y Galbán.

The central altarpiece, inset between marble and bronze columns, has a white marble relief of *The Apparition of the Virgin to Saint James of Compostela,* by Juan Adán. Above is a broken pediment with little

The Museum Door.
In the page before: the Main Façade.

Museo

angels bearing an Archbishop's cross. On both sides, above the altar tables, are further marble reliefs, also by Juan Adán, depicting *Saint Jerome* and *Saint Isidore.*

On the left side is a marble altar with a sculpture of *Saint Anthony,* again by Adán, while on the right is the tomb and the image of *Archbishop Jorge in prayer.*

3. Saint Jerome's Door. This was closed up to create a secondary sacristy. It is now a chapel with an image of the *Crucified Christ* by Pablo de Rojas, as well as other paintings and sculptures.

4. The Chapel of Our Lady Carmen. In the middle of the chapel is a Baroque altarpiece made to house various sculptures originally in the Carmen Convent in Granada; at the base is an urn with the image of *The dead Saint Casilda* (by an artist of the circle of Torcuato Ruiz del Peral); in the centre is an image intended to be dressed of *The Carmen Virgin,* attributed to José de Mora; on the right is *Saint Simón Stock*, and on the left a *Saint Elias* by Pedro de Mena. Above the main image is a reliquary case with relics of the Passion.

On each side of the altar on brackets are images of *Saint Teresa* and *Saint John of the Cross.*

On the marble side altars are two large paintings by Luis Sanz of 1770, representing *Saint Anthony* on the left and *Saint Pedro de Alcántara* on the right.

5. The Chapel of Our Lady of Sorrows. This chapel contains the altar made by José de Bada between 1737 and 1741 and originally intended for the retrochoir. It is made of red marble inlaid with other marbles of various colours. In the central niche is the image of *the Virgin of Sorrows* in grey and white marble; at her feet are two small, weeping angels. In the other niches are images of the *bishops Saint Cecilius, Saint Gregorio Bético, Saint Tomás de Villanueva* and *Saint Pedro Pascual.* The sculptures were made by Agustín Vera Moreno.

On the left wall is an image of *Saint Sebastian*, and on the right one of *Saint Louis, Bishop of Toulouse*. Above this image is a canvas of *Christ the Saviour* by Risueño.

The light entering the chapel is filtered through three modern stained glass windows (the central one depicting *The Annunciation*).

6. The Pardon Door. (page 28)

7. The Chapel of the Virgin Antigua. This chapel has a Baroque altarpiece commissioned by Archbishop Martín Ascargorta in 1716 and completed two years later to a design by Pedro Duque Cornejo. In a large central niche beneath a canopy imitating cloth, is a fifteenth-century German sculpture of *The Virgin with the Infant Christ in her arms*. On each side are figures of *Saints Cecilius* and *Gregorio Bético*. In the lower level are four small canvases (depicting *The Birth of the Virgin, The Annunciation to the Shepherds, The Visitation* and *The Annunciation*) and a series of high reliefs representing *Scenes from the Life of the Virgin*. In the upper part are reliefs of *The four Evangelists* and crowning the whole are the *Archangels Michael* in the centre with *Raphael and Gabriel* on either side. Behind the angels are

The Chapel of Our Lady of Sorrows.

three windows inset into the altarpiece itself. Seated on the volutes at the outer edges are two children.

On the side walls of the chapel are two large arches with *Portraits of the Catholic Kings*, painted by Francisco Alonso Argüello in 1649.

8. The Chapel of Saint Lucy. The central altar is a work by Gaspar Guerrero. It is framed by a semi-circular arch made of plaster with two trumpet-playing angels. In the central opening is a sculpture of *Saint Lucy* by Alonso de Mena; on the right is one of *Saint Ferdinand* by the same sculptor; on the left is a *Saint Roch* by the School of Rojas. At the top of the altarpiece is a semicircular pediment with an image of *God the Father*.

The side altars are more Baroque in style; both are topped by vases of lilies. On the right altar is a sculpture of *Saint Louis*; on the left an image of *Saint Francisco de Borja*.

On the left of the altarpiece is an image of *Christ at the Column* which dates from the sixteenth century but has been extensively restored.

9. The Chapel of the Suffering Christ. This chapel includes a small altarpiece with scenes from *The Passion* dating from the sixteenth century but largely repainted. Above the entablature is a relief of *The Burial of Christ* and above the volutes two small praying figures. The altarpiece is topped by a pediment with an image of *God the Father*.

To the left of the altar on a bracket is a fifteenth-century German sculpture of *The Virgin of the Guide* (the face redone in the eighteenth century). On a bracket on the left is a sculpture of *Saint John the Baptist* by the Circle of Risueño.

10. The Chapel of Saint Teresa. The altar was made by Gaspar Guerrero in 1618 to house an image of *Saint Teresa* donated by the Barefoot Carmelites. This takes up the middle of the altarpiece which also has five paintings with *Scenes from the life of the saint*, painted between 1620 and 1622 and attributed to the Carmelite monk Adriano.

On the side altars in important frames are two canvases by Juan de Sevilla: an *Immaculate Conception* on the left, and *The Guardian Angel* on the right.

11. The Chapel of Saint Blas. This has a small Baroque altar of only one storey, topped by a sort of attic level. In the niche is a sculpture of *Saint Blas with a child at his feet*, by an artist of the circle of Alonso de Mena.

There are two paintings by Juan de Sevilla: a *Saint Jerome* and a *Saint Onophrius*.

12. The Chapel of Saint Cecilius. This Neo-classical chapel was designed by Francisco Aguado at the end of the eighteenth century and decorated by Miguel de Verdiguier. It is lined with white marble and bronzes and is a rather cold and expressionless space.

The main altar is larger and more elaborate than the side ones. It has an image of *Saint Cecilius* and above the pediment, *Saint Indalecio*, *Saint Torcuato* and a *Representation of Faith*. The altarpiece on the right has a representation of *Saint John of God* and on

The Chapel of the Virgin Antigua.

the pediment an *Allegory of Charity*. The left altarpiece has a *Saint Emigdio* and on the pediment an *Allegory of Protection*.

All the sculptures are by Miguel Verdiguier, as are the angels and the other reliefs that decorate the walls.

13. The Chapel of Saint Sebastian. This Baroque altarpiece has a large canvas depicting *The Martyrdom of Saint Sebastian*, by Juan de Sevilla. Beneath, in a niche, is a small seventeenth-century sculpture of a saint; at the sides are depictions of *Saint Barbara* (by an artist close to Risueño) and *Saint Roch* (by the Circle of Pablo de Rojas).

On the walls, on plinths, are two terracotta sculptures of *The Infant Christ*.

14. The Chapel of Saint Ann. The altarpiece is by Gaspar Guerrero; it dates from 1615 and is in the transitional style between Renaissance and Baroque. The central niche is decorated with angels and has sculptures of *Saints Ann with the Virgin and Child*, all by Diego Pesquera.

The rest of the altarpiece is decorated with eight canvases on sea subjects, all by Pedro de Raxis.

On each side of the central altarpiece hang two paintings (*Saint Christopher* and *Saint John Nepomuk*) by Luis de Sanz.

The paintings on the side altars depict *Saint Felix of Valois* and *Saint Juan de Mata* and are by Atanasio Bocanegra.

15. The Ecce Homo or School Door. (page 28)

16. The Sacristy Door and the Sacristy. The doorway of the Sacristy was made between 1530 and 1534 by Diego de Siloé. It is of semi-circular arch form, framed by two pilasters with balustraded columns. The spandrels are decorated with trumpet-playing angels. Above the cornice, which is decorated with grotesque work, are two pedestals supporting the figures of *Saint Peter* and *Saint Paul*, and in the centre is a tondo with a relief of *The Virgin and Child*. In the cartouche above is an inscription in Latin, reading: "This is the place of the holy vestments. Cast off, o priest, the trappings of the old man and re-clothe thyself in Christ".

The **Sacristy** is a modest room built in the second half of the eighteenth century to replace a temporary one that was destroyed in a fire. In the Ante-sacristy are 36 walnut cupboards for the priests' vestments. On the walls are paintings, notably *a Holy Family* by Juan de Sevilla. In the Sacristy, above the walnut cabinets, are eight French mirrors in gilded frames. On the main wall is a magnificent sculpture of *The Crucified Christ* (possibly by Martínez Montañes), and below this, the most precious small object in the cathedral, a sculpture of *The Immaculate Virgin* by Alonso Cano.

Next to the Sacristy is a small private room for prayer of square groundplan with a vault that terminates in an octagonal lantern, the whole decorated with stucco work. The room houses an altarpiece made to house a painting of *The Immaculate Conception* by Cano (a replica of his famous sculpted image), and to house the cathedral's relics. From its style and technique, the altarpiece would seem to be by Pedro Duque Cornejo.

The Sacristy.

17. The Altarpiece of Saint James of Compostela. This Baroque altarpiece was designed by Francisco Hurtado Izquierdo and made by Juan de la Torre in 1707.

In the centre on a large platform, is a sculpture of *The Apostle James on horseback* by Alonso de Mena (donated to the cathedral by the City in 1640). Above and behind him, beneath a little canopy, is a painting of *The Virgin*, given by Pope Innocent VIII to Queen Isabel the Catholic. On either side are sculptures of *Saint Cecilius* by José de Mora, and *Saint Gregorio Bético* by Diego de Mora. In the upper part are two oval canvases of *Saint Tomás de Villanueva and Saint Pedro Pascual* by José Risueño; and, in the centre, in a niche, a sculpture of *The Immaculate Virgin*, probably also by Risueño.

Buried in front of the altar is Archbishop Martín de Ascargorta, commemorated in a marble plaque on the right.

18. The Doorway of the Royal Chapel. The main entrance of the Royal Chapel was designed by Enrique Egas and made by Jorge Fernández in 1527.

Built in the Florid Gothic style, it consists of a semi-circular festooned arch in whose jambs are sculptures of *Saint John the Baptist* and *Saint John the Evangelist* (the dedicatory saints of the chapel in honour of the fathers of Isabel of Ferdinand, both of whom were called Juan). Six small sculptures of *Seated Apostles* between canopies and brackets decorate the archivolt. On the side pilasters are two *Kings in armour* wearing emblasoned tunics. Above the door is the coat-of-arms of the Catholic Kings and to its sides the yoke and the arrows. Above is a relief of *The Adoration of the Magi* and at the sides *Saint George* (patron saint of Aragon) and *Saint James of Compostela* (patron saint of Spain).

At each side of the door, on the flanking pilasters, Siloé placed two large *shields* with the arms of the Catholic Kings and of Charles V, supported by angels.

19. The Altarpiece of Christ the Nazarene. This large altarpiece is of complex Baroque design. It was designed by Marcos Fernández in 1722 and made by Félix Rodríguez and José Narvaéz with the gilding by Francisco Moreno. It was constructed to house in a rather random manner ten canvases of different sizes and varying artistic merit. Alonso Cano painted *The Christ bearing the Cross* (the best of the ten), *The Virgin, the Saviour*, and *Saint Augustin*. Ribera painted *Saint Anthony, Saint Lawrence, The Magdalen, Saint Peter* and *Saint Paul the Hermit* (the original was stolen in 1842). The canvas of *Saint Francis of Assisi* was erroneously attributed to El Greco.

20. The Chapel of the Holy Trinity. In the centre of this chapel is a gilded wooden altarpiece designed to house various paintings. The lower layer has two paintings on copper by Italian artists (depicting *The Virgin and Child and Saint Anthony*); in the main level are three canvases by Carlo Maratta (depicting *The Descent from the Cross, The Death of Saint Joseph,* and *The Marriage of the Virgin*); in the second level is a sketch by Alonso Cano (*The Holy Trinity*), and four canvases by Maratta (two

The Door of the Royal Chapel.

of *The Virgin, The Magdalen and Saint Francis*).

The altar on the left has a canvas of *Saint Joseph with the Christ Child* which is a copy of a painting by Ribera. The right altar has a painting of *Saint Francisco de Paula*, and copy of a Ribera.

On the walls of this chapel are paintings of *The Last Supper* (sixteenth century), a Flemish copy of *The Divine Shepherdess*, a *Saint Peter* (seventeenth century), two cornucopia with canvases of *Saint John the Baptist and Saint Anthony*, an *Immaculate Virgin*, and a *Holy Family*. In addition, on both sides of the altar on pedestals are two polychrome wooden sculptures of *Saint Louis the Bishop* by Pablo de Rojas, and *Saint Joseph with the Christ Child* from the circle of Felipe González.

21. The Doorway leading to the adjacent Church. In the entrance porch are paintings from a *Series of the Apostles*. On the left wall is a painted representation of a very popular devotional image known as *Christ of the Cloth*, and on the right wall is a painting of *Christ the Nazarene*, before which Saint John of God would pray.

22. The Chapel of Saint Michael. This Neo-classical chapel was decorated by Francisco Romero de Aragón between 1804 and 1807 and was the funerary chapel of Archbishop Juan Manuel Moscoso (died 24 July 1811).

In between serpentine columns with bronze capitals and pedestals (chased by Narcisco Miguel Bueno) the central altarpiece has a relief of *The Archangel Michael* in white marble by Juan Adán and is crowned by *A Trinity group* by Manuel González.

On the right, a white marble altar flanked by serpentine columns frames a painting of *The Virgin Dolorosa* by Alonso Cano. On the left is the white marble tomb of Archbishop Moscoso by Jaime Folch. Above the tomb is a canvas of *The Virgin "Purísima"* by a Sevillian school artist.

The fresco paintings on the walls and ceiling were painted by Vicente Plaza de Loya.

23. The Door of Refuge. This doorway was executed in 1699 and is of similar structure and dimensions to the Tower Doorway.

The Exterior

The East Façade

This corresponds to the outside of the sanctuary. It faces onto a street that is so narrow that it is impossible to appreciate its impressive construction. This façade has a small door called the **Ecce Homo Door,** designed by Siloé and executed by Sancho del Cerro in 1530. It is also known as the "School Door" as it was the way into a church school belonging to the Chapter.

The North Façade

There are two doors on this side, the Pardon Door and Saint Jerome's Door

The Pardon Door is made up of two elements built at different periods. The first is a masterpiece by Siloé and was completed in 1537. It is of arch form, flanked by large striated columns on pedestals with Plateresque decoration in the jambs, the soffits and the top. In the pendentives of the

The Pardon Door.

arch are the figures of *Faith and Justice* mentioned earlier, holding up a cartouche. On the side buttresses are two large shields held up by angels; the left is the *coat-of-arms of the Catholic Kings*, that on the right *the arms of Charles V*. The second level was built in 1616 by Ambrosio Vico following the basic design of the first part but with minimal decoration. In the central part of the arch is a relief of *God the Father*, while the pendentives have figures of *King David* on the left and *The prophet Jeremiah* on the right (both probably by Martín de Aranda). The relief of *The Incarnation* intended for the centre was left unfinished.

Saint Jerome's Door is made up of two sections. The lower section, executed by Siloé in 1532, is an arch with two Corinthian pilasters decorated with Plasteresque motifs, with tondos in the pendentives and a simple cartouche above the keystone. The second level was constructed by Maeda, roughly following the earlier part. In the niche is a relief of *Saint Jerome in penitence* which is probably by Diego de Pesquera. Above is an oculus flanked by anthropomorphic figures and two vases of lilies. In the upper part is a cartouche held up by angels and dated 1639. The **Tower** consists of three levels (it had a further octagonal one, but this had to be dismantled in 1590 just after it was built as it threatened to pull down the whole structure.) The first section was built by Siloé. The decoration of the walls that close the arches of the second level can be attributed to Vico. The tri-partite windows of the bell-tower section seem to have been designed by Asensio de Maeda. There are 16 bells in the tower.

The West Façade. The Main Façade

Siloé had intended to build a façade with two twin towers on each side, but this was substituted for the design by Alonso Cano, built by José Granados. It consists of a colossal, triple triumphal arch (the central opening wider and higher), divided into three levels by a simple cornice. At the beginning of the eighteenth century, two consoles were placed on either side of the central door to support sculptures of *Saints Peter and Paul* (attributed to Duque Cornejo), with the further addition above the archway of this door of a high relief of *The Incarnation*, made in 1717 by José Risueño. The remaining sculptures (the *statues* above the cornice *representing the Old Testament, The New Testament and Saints Michael* and *Raphael*), the low reliefs of *The Visitation* and *The Assumption* above the side doors, and the medallions with reliefs of *The Evangelists* which serve as capitals to the pilasters of the first level, are all by the French sculptor Miguel Verdiguier and his son Luis Pedro, and were made between 1782 and 1783. Stained glass was added to the skylights in 1884, made by the Mayer workshop in Munich.

The spire to the right of the façade acts as a counterbalance to the great mass of the tower. It is topped with a sculpture of *The Archangel Michael.*

The South Façade

This adjoins the Royal Chapel and the Sagrarium Church, the latter built between 1705 and 1759 on the site formerly occupied by the mosque and which, after its demolition, had been destined for use as the cathedral cloister.

The Tower.